First Facts®

LEARN ABOUT ANIMAL BEHAVIOR

ANIMAL MIGRATION

BY JEANIE MEBANE

Consultant:
Bernd Heinrich, PhD
Department of Biology
University of Vermont, Burlington

CAPSTONE PRESS
a capstone imprint

First Facts is published by Capstone Press,
1710 Roe Crest Drive, North Mankato, Minnesota 56003.
www.capstonepub.com

Library of Congress Cataloging-in-Publication Data
Mebane, Jeanie.
Animal migration / by Jeanie Mebane.
p. cm. — (First facts. Learn about animal behavior)
Includes bibliographical references and index.
Summary: "Discusses the animal behavior of migration"—Provided by publisher.
ISBN 978-1-4296-8267-1 (library binding)
ISBN 978-1-4296-9306-6 (paperback)
ISBN 978-1-62065-256-5 (ebook PDF)
1. Animal migration—Juvenile literature. I. Title.
QL754.M43 2013
591.56'8—dc23   2012002118

Editorial Credits
Christine Peterson, editor; Alison Thiele, designer; Svetlana Zhurkin, media researcher;
    Laura Manthe, production specialist

Photo Credits
Alamy: Jeff Mondragon, 21; Dreamstime: Karin Van Ijzendoorn, 5, Oleg Znamenskiy, cover,
Paul Banton, 9, Scol22, cover (inset), back cover, 1, Tony Campbell, 17, Tracey Taylor, 15; Minden
Pictures: Norbert Wu, 10; National Geographic Stock: Greg Winston, 6; Shutterstock: Eliks
(background), throughout, Lynn Human, 14, Mikhail Levit, 18, Steve Byland, 13, therocketbaby
(zebra pattern), throughout

Essential content terms are **bold** and are defined at the bottom of the spread where
they first appear.

Printed in the United States of America in North Mankato, Minnesota.
042012   006682CGF12

TABLE OF
CONTENTS

What Is Migration?

How are some zebras, whales, and birds alike? They all migrate between **habitats** two or more times a year. Animals move to find food or shelter or to have young. They travel over land, through water, or by air. Migrating isn't easy. During their journey, animals face hunger, **predators**, and other dangers.

habitat: the natural place and conditions in which a plant or animal lives

predator: an animal that hunts other animals for food

Land Migration

Animals migrate across the land using routes their ancestors have followed for years. Pronghorn graze in Wyoming's Grand Teton National Park all summer. In winter, snow buries their food. To survive, pronghorn travel south where food is easier to find. They return to their northern home in spring.

Animal Fact!
Pronghorns walk about 150 miles (240 kilometers) to reach their winter home.

Moving in Herds

Many animals migrate in groups to stay safe from predators. Huge herds of African wildebeests migrate four times a year seeking fresh grass. They travel about 1,800 miles (2,900 km) a year. But their trip can be dangerous. If chased by predators, wildebeest herds gallop for short distances. Their hooves pound the ground and raise thick dust clouds. The dust hides them from danger.

Animal Fact!

More than 1.4 million wildebeests migrate across parts of Africa.

Migrating in Water

Sea animals migrate too. Gray whales live in northern waters all summer. They feast on **zooplankton**. In fall food becomes scarce. Then whales move south. It can take up to four months for whales to reach warm, tropical waters. At their winter home, female whales give birth to young. When food grows hard to find, whales move north again.

zooplankton: tiny sea creatures

Strong Flyers

Millions of birds and colorful butterflies migrate through the air. Butterflies and birds fly high in the air where wind currents help them move.

Ruby-throated hummingbirds spend summers in the United States and Canada. They eat insects and suck nectar from flowers. Each fall they migrate to Central America. They fly nonstop for more than 30 hours across the Gulf of Mexico.

Animal Fact! Some hummingbirds return to the same flowering bush they visited a year earlier.

Preparing for the Trip

Whether by land, water, or air, all animals must prepare for their trip. Some animals gain weight. Fat provides fuel for migrating. Monarch butterflies add fat by sipping nectar.

Birds **molt** old, worn feathers before migrating. They grow strong, new ones. These new feathers help birds like whooper swans fly long distances. Whoopers fly more than 800 miles (1,300 km) without resting.

molt: shedding fur, feathers, or an outer layer of skin

Stops along the Way

Migrating animals take breaks to rest and eat. Sandhill cranes spend the winter in southern U.S. states. In spring they fly to the northern United States or Canada. More than 500,000 cranes stop along the Platte River in Nebraska. They stay nearly a month, eating grain left in fields. This food gives them energy to continue their trip.

Finding the Way

Migrating animals don't have maps or GPS units. Instead, animals use their **senses** and memories to find routes. Some animals use the earth's **magnetic field** as a guide. Others follow landmarks such as mountains, rivers, and coasts. Some use echoes and ocean waves to find their way. Birds use the sun, moon, and stars as guides.

sense: a way of knowing about your surroundings
magnetic field: an area of moving electrical currents that affects other objects

Studying Migration

Scientists study migration to help animals. By knowing how animals migrate, people can protect them and their routes. Some scientists track animals from airplanes. Some use satellite cameras. Others attach tracking radios to animals. The radios send back messages that show the animals' routes.

Animal Fact!

People also tag butterflies, band birds, and watch migrations. Scientists use this information to track animals.

Amazing but True!

If you were thousands of miles from home, could you find your way back? Pacific salmon can. Salmon hatch in freshwater streams and live in the ocean for years.

When it is time to lay their eggs, the salmon migrate. They go back to the same stream where they hatched! Some travel more than 2,000 miles (3,220 km). Scientists think salmon may use their sense of smell to find the right stream.

Glossary

ancestor (AN-ses-tuhr)—a member of a person's or animal's family who lived a long time ago

habitat (HAB-uh-tat)—the natural place and conditions in which a plant or animal lives

magnetic field (mag-NET-ic FEELD)—an area of moving electrical currents that affects other objects

molt (MOHLT)—shedding fur, feathers, or an outer layer of skin; after molting a new covering grows

predator (PRED-uh-tur)—an animal that hunts other animals for food.

sense (SENSS)—a way of knowing about your surroundings; hearing, smelling, touching, tasting, and sight are the five senses

zooplankton (zoh-PLANK-ton)—tiny sea creatures that drift in huge numbers

Read More

Brynie, Faith Hickman. *Do Animals Migrate?* I Like Reading about Animals! Berkeley Heights, N.J.: Enslow Publishers, 2010.

Carney, Elizabeth. *Great Migrations: Whales, Wildebeests, Butterflies, Elephants, and Other Amazing Animals on the Move.* National Geographic Kids. Washington D.C.: National Geographic, 2010.

Kalman, Bobbie. *Why Do Animals Migrate?* Big Science Ideas. New York: Crabtree Pub., 2009.

Internet Sites

FactHound offers a safe, fun way to find Internet sites related to this book. All of the sites on FactHound have been researched by our staff.

Here's all you do:

Visit *www.facthound.com*

Type in this code: 9781429682671

Check out projects, games and lots more at
www.capstonekids.com

Index